Christianity, Cults & Religions
Participant Guide

Paul Carden

BEN

This Participant Guide accompanies the

Christianity, Cults & Religions 6-Session DVD-Based Study

(ISBN 9781596364134 or 9781596364271)

with

Christianity, Cults & Religions Leader Guide

(ISBN 9781596364288)

Containing: Glossary of Words, Definitions of Concepts, Activity Sheets, Charts

ROSE
PUBLISHING

© 2010 Bristol Works, Inc.
Rose Publishing, Inc.
4733 Torrance Blvd., #259
Torrance, California 90503 U.S.A.
Email: info@rose-publishing.com
www.rose-publishing.com

Celtic cross photo ©Pears2295

Scripture quotations marked "NASB" are taken from the *New American Standard Bible*, © Copyright 1960, 1962, 1963, 1968, 1971, 1972, 1973, 1975, 1977, 1995 by The Lockman Foundation. Used by permission.
Scripture quotations marked "NIV" are taken from the *Holy Bible, New International Version*®. NIV®. Copyright © 1973, 1978, 1984 by International Bible Society. Used by permission of Zondervan. All rights reserved.

Printed in the United States of America

Contents

About the Complete Christianity, Cults & Religions DVD-Based Kit
(ISBN 9781596364134)

The Kit includes everything you need to teach *Christianity, Cults & Religions*, using professionally-produced video sessions and a PowerPoint® presentation. The Complete Kit includes:

- DVD with 6 teaching sessions

- One printed *Christianity, Cults & Religions Participant Guide* (ISBN 9781596364295)

- One printed *Christianity, Cults & Religions Leader Guide* (ISBN 9781596364288) + PDF Leader Guide

- One printed *Rose Bible Basics: Christianity, Cults & Religions* handbook (ISBN 9781596362024)

- One *Christianity, Cults & Religions* pamphlet comparing 20 religions and cults side by side (ISBN 9789901981403)

- *Christianity, Cults & Religion* PowerPoint® presentation on CD-ROM (ISBN 9781890947323)

- PDF files for posters, fliers, handouts and bulletin inserts for promotion

Available at www.ChristianityCultsandReligions.com or
www.rose-publishing.com, or by calling Rose Publishing at
1-800-532-4278. Also available wherever good Christian books are sold.

About This Study

As Christians living in the 21st century, we are faced with increasing religious diversity and religious competition. In this ever-shrinking world, people in cults and other religions may be showing up on your doorstep, at your job, or maybe even in your own family. You might be wondering, How can I possibly "always be prepared to give an answer" (1 Peter 3:15)?

We should take our cue from the apostle Paul who skillfully employed his knowledge of pagan philosophies to evangelize unbelievers (Acts 17:16–34). To witness in today's world, Christians need a basic understanding of what cults and religions teach, so they can know how to relate to people in various religious groups.

In this study, Paul Carden explains the essential teachings of popular cults and major religions. But he also takes you beneath the surface to shed light on what really attracts and keeps people in these religious groups. Each session lays out a solid Scriptural foundation for discerning the truth and dispels common misconceptions and stereotypes. But above all, this study is here to help you think biblically, so you can evangelize with compassion, clarity, and confidence.

About the Author

For more than 30 years, Paul Carden has been a leading researcher of religions, cults, and new religious movements. For six years, he co-hosted the live, nationwide *Bible Answer Man* radio broadcast alongside Ron Rhodes, Robert M. Bowman Jr., and other noted apologists. He joined Christian Research Institute and was the director of International Outreach under its founder, Walter Martin. He has also served as a senior editor of the *Christian Research Journal* and has spent six years as a missionary in Brazil.

Today he is the executive director of the Centers for Apologetics Research, an organization that monitors and researches religions and cults around the world. His passion for evangelism and educating Christians is evident. He brings to this study his extensive experience in training believers how to effectively witness to people in cults and world religions.

He and his wife, Lisa, have four children and live in San Juan Capistrano, California.

Definitions, Discernment, and Defending the Faith

Some things you will learn in this session...

- How to identify false teachers—"wolves in sheep's clothing."

- How heresy subverts the truth.

- The reasons why people are drawn into cults—and why it's so hard to leave.

- Which beliefs cults most often distort.

Follow Along and Take Notes

Session 1 Outline
Definitions, Discernment, and Defending the Faith

1. Scriptural foundation

    a. Matthew 28:19

    b. Jude 3 4

    c. Matthew 24:4–5, 11, 24

    d. Acts 20:28–31a

    e. 2 Corinthians 11:3–4

    f. Galatians 1:6, 9

2. Practical definitions

    a. What is a religion?

    b. What is a cult?

    c. What is a heresy?

3. Six categories of false teaching:

    a. Revelation

    b. God

    c. Jesus Christ

    d.   Salvation

    e.   The church

    f.   The future

4. Why are people drawn into cults?

    a.   The tactics used to recruit, convert, and hold members

    b.   The personal vulnerability of the potential recruit

        • Proverbs 27:7; 14:12

5. How can we respond?

    a.   Have a mature grasp of Scripture

        • Hebrews 5:14; Ephesians 4:14

    b.   Be vigilant

        • 1 Thessalonians 5:21–22

        • 1 John 4:1

        • Acts 17:11

    c.   Practice caring outreach

        • 2 Timothy 2:25

Key Terms

Religion   "A set of beliefs that answers the ultimate questions. What is ultimate reality? What is the nature of the world? What is the nature of humanity? What is humanity's primary problem? What happens after death?" (Dean Halverson, *The Illustrated Guide to World Religions*; Bethany, 2003; p. 10)

"Any socially organized pattern of beliefs and practices concerning ultimate meaning that assumes the existence of the supernatural." (Rodney Stark, quoted in Irving Hexham, *Concise Dictionary of Religion*; IVP, 1993; p. 187)

Heresy   "A teaching which directly opposes the essentials of the Christian faith, so that true Christians must divide themselves from all those who hold it." (Robert M. Bowman, Jr., *Orthodoxy and Heresy: A Biblical Guide to Doctrinal Discernment*; Baker, 1992; p. 50)

"It is a Trojan horse, a means of establishing (whether by accident or design) an alternative belief system within its host. Heresy appears to be Christian, but it is actually an enemy of faith that sows the seed of faith's destruction." (Alister McGrath, *Heresy: A History of Defending the Truth*; HarperOne, 2009; p. 34)

Cult   "An ideological organization held together by charismatic relationships and demanding total commitment." (Benjamin Zablocki, quoted in Herbert L. Rosedale and Michael D. Langone, *"On Using the Term 'Cult'"*)

"A religious group originating as a heretical sect and maintaining fervent commitment to heresy." (Robert M. Bowman, Jr., *Orthodoxy and Heresy: A Biblical Guide to Doctrinal Discernment*; Baker, 1992; p. 115)

A cult of Christianity would be "a group of people, which claiming to be Christian, embraces a particular doctrinal system taught by an individual leader, group of leaders, or organization, which [system] denies (either explicitly or implicitly) one or more of the central doctrines of the Christian faith." (Alan Gomes as quoted in Ron Rhodes, *The Challenge of the Cults and New Religions*; Zondervan, 2001; p. 22)

Talk About It

Discussion Questions

1. Why is it important for Christians to learn about other religions?

2. What is discernment? And how does a Christian grow in discernment?

3. What does it mean to "defend the faith"? Give some examples of what defending the faith might look like.

4. After watching the first session, what are you excited about learning in this study?

5. What questions do you still have about this study?

Get Into God's Word

Key Bible Verses

Read Matthew 7:15–20

Q   What does Jesus warn us about? And how can we recognize danger?

_____

_____

_____

Read 1 John 4:1–4

Q   How does John assure believers that they can resist being deceived?

_____

_____

_____

Read 2 Timothy 2:24–26

Q   According to this passage, what should we do about those who oppose sound teaching?

_____

_____

_____

Test Your Knowledge

Quick Quiz

1. According to the session, what is heresy?

    a. Teachings found in the Christian creeds.
    b. Teachings that oppose the essentials of the Christian faith.
    c. Any teaching not contained in a church's statement of faith.
    d. Anything I disagree with.

2. True or False? The people who join cults are usually social misfits with little education and have difficulty holding a job.

3. According to this session, what draws people into cults?

    a. Looking for solace during an emotionally vulnerable time in life.
    b. The "love" they feel from cult leaders.
    c. The false promises that cult leaders make.
    d. (a) and (b)
    e. All of the above

4. True or False? Cults often use Christian vocabulary, but redefine the terms to mean something very different.

5. According to this session, the four points derived from Jude 3–4 are: (1) There is one faith; (2) That faith is unchanging; (3) We are to earnestly contend for the faith; and (4) The faith has_____.

(Answers on page 94)

Think About It

Personal Reflection

1. How do I practice discernment in my spiritual life?

_____

_____

_____

2. What can I do to learn how to better defend the faith?

_____

_____

_____

3. Whom do I know that may be falling prey to false beliefs or getting involved in a cultic group? How should I speak with them? How should I pray for them?

_____

_____

_____

Notes

Essential Christian Doctrine

Some things you will learn in this session....

- Why Christianity is unique among all the world religions.

- How the Bible compares to other religious writings.

- What other religious groups say about Jesus.

- How to recognize the counterfeit claims of cults.

Session 2 Outline
Essential Christian Doctrine

1. The standard

    a. General revelation (nature)

        - Psalm 19

        - Romans 1:20

    b. Special revelation (Scripture)

        - 2 Peter 1:21

        - 2 Timothy 3:16

2. Heresy and orthodoxy

    a. Heresy

    b. Orthodoxy

3. Four universal creeds

    a. Apostles' Creed

    b. Nicene Creed

    c. Athanasian Creed

    d.   Definition of Chalcedon

4.   A dozen essential doctrines

    a.   God's unity

- Deuteronomy 6:4

- 1 Corinthians 8:5–6

    b.   The Trinity

- 2 Thessalonians 1:2

- John 1:1

- Matthew 28:19

    c.   Human depravity

- Romans 3:9–20

- John 3:3

    d.   The virgin birth

- Luke 1:34–35, Matthew 1:18

    e.   The sinlessness of Christ

- Hebrews 4:15

- 1 Peter 2:22

- 2 Corinthians 5:21

f.   Christ's deity...

g.   ...and Christ's humanity

  • John 1:14

  • Hebrews 1:1–8

  • Galatians 4:4–5

  • 1 John 4:2–3

h.   God's grace

  • Romans 5:10

  • Titus 3:5

i.   Faith

  • Ephesians 2:8–9

j.   Christ's atoning death

  • Romans 3:25–26

k.   Jesus' bodily resurrection

  • 1 Corinthians 15:1–6

l.   Christ's second coming

  • Acts 1:11

  • Revelation 1:7

Key Terms

Confession (from Latin *confiteri*, "acknowledge") Like creeds, confessions are an active acknowledgement of the church's faith and teachings. "Confessions of faith" often include both creedal declarations and statements summarizing the distinctive teachings of a particular denomination or group of believers.

Creed (from Latin *credo*, "I believe") A simple summary of beliefs. Creeds are easy to memorize and flexible to teach.

Doctrine (from Latin *doctrina*, "teaching," "learning") A belief that a group holds as true. Christian doctrines organize and explain the beliefs the church learns from the Bible.

Heresy (from Greek *hairesis*, "choice," "faction") A teaching that contradicts another teaching that has been accepted as the norm; the opposite of orthodoxy.

Orthodoxy (from Greek *ortho*, "straight," and *doxa*, "belief, opinion") The opposite of heresy. Irenaeus (AD 130–200) used the word orthodox to characterize his own teachings, with which most other Church Fathers agreed, and the word heresy to define those of his adversaries. When Orthodox is capitalized (as in Greek Orthodox, Russian Orthodox) it refers to the church bodies of Eastern Europe and the Middle East that divided from the churches aligned with Rome in the Great Schism of AD 1054.

Talk About It

Discussion Questions

1. Which essential doctrines do you think are easiest for people to accept? Which ones are most difficult? Why?

2. Which essential doctrines do you notice cults denying or distorting most often?

3. How does understanding the "bad news" of human depravity help us appreciate the "good news" of Jesus Christ?

4. What is the significance of Jesus' bodily resurrection?

5. If someone were to ask you, "What is grace?" what would you say?

Get Into God's Word

Key Bible Verses

℘ Read John 1:1–14.

Q Jesus Christ is referred to in this passage as "the Word." What does this passage reveal about who Jesus Christ was and is?

_____

_____

_____

℘ Read 1 Corinthians 15:1–6

Q In your own words, what is the "gospel" that the apostle Paul is reminding his readers of in this passage?

_____

_____

_____

Test Your Knowledge

Quick Quiz

1. The creeds help believers to:

    a. Recognize heresy.
    b. Distinguish essentials from nonessentials.
    c. Express the faith clearly.
    d. (a) and (b)
    e. All of the above.

2. True or False? Mary Baker Eddy, the founder of Christian Science, taught that sin, sickness, and death are unreal.

3. The Bible is:

    a. Divinely inspired.
    b. Preserved by God.
    c. A collection of opinions.
    d. (a) and (b)
    e. All of the above

4. True or False? Mormonism teaches that God has always been God.

5. The Bible teaches in Ephesians 2:8–9 that it is by_____ through faith that we are saved—and that is not from ourselves.

(Answers on page 94)

Think About It

Personal Reflection

1. Choose one (or two or more!) of the key Bible verses or any of the Scripture references mentioned in this session to memorize. Memorizing Bible verses will not only be personally edifying, but will be useful to recall on-the-spot when you are in conversation with someone in a cult or another religion.

    _____

    _____

    _____

    _____

2. Read the creeds. You can find the texts of the four ecumenical (universal) creeds, as well as various denominational statements of belief, at www.creeds.net. Ask yourself, What does the creed explain about God? How can I use this teaching to discern the truth?

    _____

    _____

    _____

    _____

Where Did the Creeds Come From?

THE APOSTLES' CREED

The apostles did not write the Apostles' Creed. No one knows for certain when this creed as written. References to and quotation of similar statements—known as the "Rule of Faith"—can be found in writings as early as the second century AD. The name "Apostles' Creed" means that the creed contains the Apostolic tradition. The Apostles' Creed is the most universal of all the creeds. Most Christian denominations continue to recite and teach it.

THE NICENE CREED

The greatest doctrinal challenge to the church arose internally. Arius, a priest in Alexandria, suggested that if God begat Jesus, then Jesus had an origin. As such, Jesus did not share in the same divine essence with the Father—making him a lesser god. This teaching became known as Arianism. In AD 325, Constantine called the leaders of the church to participate in a council—that is, an assembly of bishops. They met in the city of Nicaea, in present-day Turkey. The Council of Nicaea, made up of about 300 participants, overwhelmingly voted against the Arian teachings—ancient documents suggest that only three bishops refused to sign their agreement. The council expressed its views about God, Jesus, and the church in the Nicene Creed.

ATHANASIAN CREED

Athanasius was one of the most active opponents of Arius' teachings. His persistence and clear mind helped the church to clarify its positions and write it in a creed, the Nicene Creed. Athanasius' teachings are summarized in the Athanasian Creed. While it is likely that Athanasius did not write it, the creed contains his teachings and main ideas. The Athanasian Creed begins by affirming, "This is what the catholic [or universal] faith teaches: we worship one God in the Trinity and the Trinity in unity. We distinguish among the persons, but we do not divide the substance [or essence]." After unpacking these ideas, the creed concludes, "So that in all things, as aforesaid, the Unity in Trinity and the Trinity in Unity is to be worshipped."

DEFINITION OF CHALCEDON

Understanding the incarnation of Jesus—the embodiment of God the Son in human flesh—was one of the greatest challenges for the early church. In AD 451 the Council of Chalcedon (located in today's Turkey) provided a clear statement of the Apostolic teachings concerning Jesus. The Definition of Chalcedon made it clear that Jesus is fully God and fully human, two natures existing in perfect harmony in one person.

(Adapted from *Creeds & Heresies: Then & Now* Rose Publishing, www.rose-publishing.com)

Jehovah's Witnesses

Watchtower Bible and Tract Society

Some things you will learn in this session....

- Why the year 1914 is so important to Jehovah's Witnesses.

- Why Jehovah's Witnesses do so much door-to-door work.

- How the Watchtower controls what its members believe.

- Why Jehovah's Witnesses will not vote or salute the flag.

- Why Jehovah's Witnesses hand out so much literature—but will not accept any from you.

- What to say to Jehovah's Witnesses who come knocking on your door.

Session 3 Outline
Jehovah's Witnesses

1. Beginnings

   a. William Miller (1782–1849), Adventism

   b. Charles Taze Russell (1852–1916)

   c. Armageddon and the year 1914

   d. "Judge" Joseph Rutherford (1869–1942)

2. The Watchtower Society today

   a. Over 18 million followers

   b. The *Watchtower* and *Awake!* magazines

   c. New World Translation

   d. The 144,000; Governing Body

3. Distinctive beliefs

   a. No Trinity

      • Jesus is a lesser, created god

- The "holy spirit" is Jehovah's invisible, active force

b. Apostate "Christendom"

c. "Anointed Class" and "other sheep"

d. What is required to be saved?

- Taking in knowledge

- Obeying God's laws

- Belonging to and serving in Jehovah's one true organization

- Being loyal to Jehovah's organization

e. Witnesses have to work toward perfection

f. Prohibitions

- Refusing blood transfusions

- No celebrating holidays, birthdays, etc.

- No military service, no voting, no flag salute

4. Biblical insights

a. One God

- Isaiah 43:10

- 1 Peter 1:1–2

b. The Holy Spirit is God

- 2 Corinthians 3:17

- Acts 5:3–4

c. Jesus is God

- Isaiah 9:6

- John 8:58; Exodus 3:14

- Colossians 2:9

- John 5:18, 23

- Hebrews 1:6

d. Jesus rose physically

- John 2:19

e. Salvation is a free gift

- Romans 6:23

- Acts 16:30–31

- Titus 3:5

- Philippians 3:9

5. Do's and don'ts

   a. Do remember that Jehovah's Witnesses are real people

   b. Do be courteous and respectful

   c. Do know the Bible

   d. Do ask questions

   e. Don't assume that Jehovah's Witnesses know the Bible

   f. Don't assume that there is only one right way to witness

   g. Don't try to force them to admit they're wrong

   h. Don't just turn them away

Key Terms

144,000/"anointed class"   According to Watchtower teaching, 144,000 is the number of Christians living between Pentecost (c. AD 30) and 1935, called the "anointed class" or "little flock," who will live in heaven as spirits forever. (The other class of Christians is called the "earthly class.")

Adventism   Followers of the various movements inspired by the teachings of American preacher William Miller (1782–1849) who predicted that the second coming of Christ would take place in 1843 or 1844.

Arianism   Originated in the fourth century AD and argues that Jesus doesn't share the same essence with God, and thus does not share in the same divine nature with eternity and authority. The Nicene, Chalcedonian, and Athanasian Creeds are primarily responses to this heresy.

Armageddon   According to the Watchtower, this is the final battle between wicked mankind and Jehovah God to end world governments which brings about the establishment of Jehovah's "kingdom rule" on Paradise Earth.

Christ's "Presence"   Watchtower teaching that the second coming of Jesus already took place invisibly in 1914.

Christendom   Disparaging term used to describe "professed Christianity"—that is, all non-Jehovah's Witness religions that claim to be Christian—in contrast with "the true Christianity of the Bible." Viewed as being under Satan's control.

Jehovah   God's personal name. Nearly all other Bibles have "LORD" for God's name in the Old Testament, but the New World Translation renders it "Jehovah"— and even "restores" the divine name to the New Testament.

New World Translation (NWT)   The official Bible of the Watchtower Society. The Watchtower has stated that other English translations have "fallen victim to the power of human traditions.... Inconsistency and unreasonableness have been insinuated into the teachings of the inspired writings." (NWT 1950)

Other Sheep   Another name Jehovah's Witnesses use for the "earthly class," drawn from John 10:16.

Theocratic Kingdom   Jehovah's kingdom rule through the Watchtower Society.

Torture Stake   The Watchtower Society teaches that Jesus was executed on an upright pole or stake instead of a two-beamed cross. Jehovah's Witnesses believe that the cross is a pagan symbol and that using it in worship violates the Second Commandment's prohibition against idolatry.

Watchtower Bible and Tract Society   The Jehovah's Witness organization, which is headquartered in Brooklyn, New York. Its "Governing Body" claims to have sole spiritual authority over Jehovah's people.

Talk About It

Discussion Questions

1. Share about a conversation you had with a Jehovah's Witness. What things were discussed? Was it easy or difficult to discuss different beliefs?

2. What are some reasons why people become Jehovah's Witnesses?

3. What is required for someone to be "saved" according to Jehovah's Witness teaching? What is required according to the Bible?

4. What difficulties and challenges do you think someone might face if he or she left the Jehovah's Witnesses and became a Christian?

5. Do you feel ready to discuss your beliefs with Jehovah's Witnesses? Why or why not? What would help you feel ready?

Get Into God's Word

Key Bible Verses

ℂ *Read Colossians 2:9–10*

Q   What do these verses tell us about who Jesus is?

_____

_____

_____

ℂ *Read Romans 6:23*

Q   What is eternal life as described in this verse? What does this indicate about how salvation is received?

_____

_____

_____

ℂ *Read Philippians 3:8–9*

Q   What does righteousness not come from? Through what does it come?

_____

_____

_____

Test Your Knowledge

Quick Quiz

1. In nearly _____ places the Jehovah's Witnesses' Bible, the New World Translation, is altered to match up with Watchtower doctrines.

    a. 50
    b. 100
    c. 200
    d. 300

2. True or False? According to Watchtower teaching, only the "anointed class" of 144,000 people has the ability and the right to properly interpret the Bible.

3. According to Watchtower teaching, Jesus was the first thing Jehovah created, and Jesus began his existence as _____.

    a. Adam
    b. A perfect human
    c. Michael the Archangel
    d. The second Person of the Trinity
    e. None of the above

4. True or False? According to Watchtower teaching, Jehovah's Witnesses have assurance of salvation because they were baptized in Jehovah's "one true organization"—the Watchtower Society.

5. When talking with Jehovah's Witnesses, remember to ask _____ instead of making accusations.

(Answers on page 94)

Think About It

Personal Reflection

1. What attitude do I usually have toward Jehovah's Witnesses?

    _____

    _____

    _____

2. How have I treated Jehovah's Witnesses who have come to my door? How does God want me to treat them?

    _____

    _____

    _____

3. What can I do to be better prepared for when Jehovah's Witnesses come knocking?

    _____

    _____

    _____

4. Do I have a friend, coworker, or family member who is a Jehovah's Witness? If so, how can I be intentional about praying for them and looking for opportunities to tell them about the good news of the free gift of salvation?

    _____

    _____

    _____

Reach Out

Witnessing Tips (Do's and Don'ts)

- *Do pray before each encounter* with the Jehovah's Witnesses and invite the Holy Spirit to lead and guide the conversation. Ask him to fill their minds and hearts with the truth of his Word.

- *Don't depend on evidence and argumentation alone.* Rely on the Holy Spirit to guide you. It's the Holy Spirit's job to convict of sin, righteousness, and judgment.

- *Do approach Jehovah's Witnesses with a humble, loving attitude.* Identify with them in genuine concern, and treat them respectfully, realizing they probably wouldn't have joined had they known all the facts.

- *Don't approach them with a superior attitude*, belittle them, or act like you have something they don't.

- *Do ask the Jehovah's Witness to help you understand how to reconcile their beliefs with the Bible.* Jehovah's Witnesses are trained to teach, not to listen to you. Questions can be a powerful tool to break through their programmed responses and to get them to "think" for themselves.

- *Don't confront Jehovah's Witnesses in an argumentative manner*, trying to "teach" them. Jehovah's Witnesses believe they have "the Truth" and that you don't have anything to offer them.

- *Do challenge the Jehovah's Witnesses' trust in the Watchtower* by showing discrepancies in their own literature. Jehovah's Witnesses are not allowed to read anti-Watchtower literature, so use their literature and Scripture alone.

- *Don't engage in deep scriptural discussion too soon.* Witnesses are told they can't understand the Bible apart from Watchtower literature, so their trust in the Watchtower needs to be broken before they can begin to interpret the Bible for themselves.

- *Do pray to "Jehovah God" with Jehovah's Witnesses* and pray about personal things that are happening in their lives. Emphasize the "Father" aspect of "Jehovah" in your prayer and how he cares for you personally.

- *Don't pray to "God" or "Lord" without addressing the prayer to "Jehovah" at some point.* Jehovah's Witnesses fear that if a prayer doesn't have Jehovah's name, it may end up in Satan's hands. Also, don't ask if you can pray with them for healing of sickness (unless they approach you privately). They're taught that God doesn't "heal" today, and anything miraculous is done by Satan to deceive the unsuspecting.

- *Do tell Jehovah's Witnesses about your personal relationship with Jesus* and how he answers prayer and personally works in your life. Jehovah's Witnesses do not believe God cares as much for them as he does for the organization, so your testimony can make them hungry for a real relationship with the true God.

- *Don't try to force the Jehovah's Witness to "agree" with you.* They're not allowed to disagree with the Watchtower, so plant seeds of doubt through your questions and let the Holy Spirit do his work.

- *Do be available, persistent, and patient.* If they're asking questions, they're starting to think for themselves. This is the first step in leaving the Watchtower..

(Excerpt from *10 Q&A on Jehovah's Witnesses* Rose Publishing, www.rose-publishing.com)

Learn More

What about the 144,000?

According to the Watchtower Society, there are two very different classes of Christians. One is a special group of 144,000 people known as the "anointed class" (also called the "heavenly class," "little flock," or "faithful and discreet slave"). They lived between Pentecost (c. AD 30) and 1935, and will one day live in heaven as spirits forever. Only members of this special class...

• are part of the new covenant and have Jesus as their mediator.

• are "born again" and have "adoption" as God's children.

• are true members of the "Christian congregation," the church.

• may partake of the "memorial emblems" of Jesus' Last Supper (Communion) once a year.

• spiritually guide God's organization today and will rule from heaven over the earth.

There is also a much larger group, the "earthly class" (also called the "other sheep" or "great crowd"). This includes virtually everyone who has become a Jehovah's Witness after 1935, along with people throughout time who weren't wicked but never heard of Christ. They will have a chance to live forever as human beings in a paradise on earth.

The heavenly and earthly classes will remain eternally separated. The earthly class will never see the Father or Jesus.

But according to the Bible, there is no "two-class" system. Christ is the mediator between God and all people who are redeemed in him (1 Timothy 2:5–6). Everyone who has faith in Christ is already "born again" (1 Peter 1:3; 1 John 5:1). Everyone who knows God as Father through Jesus Christ has the "adoption as sons" (Romans 8:14–17; Galatians 4:4–6) and is his child (John 1:12–13). All baptized believers are part of the church, the body of Christ (1 Corinthians 12:13).

All true believers will live together in the new heaven and new earth. Scripture teaches that when believers in Christ die, they go immediately into God's presence (Luke 23:43; Philippians 1:21–24). All believers from all ages will be resurrected with immortal bodies like Christ's (Romans 8:11; 1 Corinthians 15:42–54; Philippians 3:21) and live together in the new heaven and new earth (Matthew 5:5; 2 Peter 3:13; Revelation 21:1). Believers in Christ will "reign on the earth" (Revelation 5:10). (Note: This "reign" may refer to God's intention for people to exercise dominion on earth [Genesis 1:26, 28] or to Christians ruling over the redeemed from past ages.) All of the redeemed will see the Father and Jesus (Matthew 5:8; 1 John 3:2; Revelation 21:3–4).

So, who are the 144,000? The Bible only refers to "144,000" in Revelation chapters 7 and 14. Christians who interpret the number literally also take the twelve Israelite tribes of 12,000 literally (Revelation 7:4–8). It makes no sense to take the number 144,000 literally but not the twelve groups of 12,000 that the text adds up to get 144,000. Christians who take the twelve tribes in this passage as symbolizing the church consistently regard the number 144,000 as symbolic. But there is no basis in Revelation 7—or any other Bible passage—for dividing Jesus' followers into two classes.

(Adapted from *10 Q&A on Jehovah's Witnesses* Rose Publishing, www.rose-publishing.com)

Traits of God and Jesus

The Watchtower teaches that Jesus is a lesser god than Jehovah. However, Scripture portrays Jesus as co-equal with God the Father, demonstrating Jesus' deity.

Traits Unique to God (Jehovah)	Traits of Jesus
Creation is "the work of his hands"—alone (Gen. 1:1; Ps. 102:25; Isa. 44:24)	Creation is "the work of his hands"—all things created in and through him (John 1:3; Col. 1:16; Heb. 1:2, 10)
"The first and the last" (Isa. 44:6)	"The first and the last" (Rev. 1:17; 22:13)
"Lord of lords" (Deut. 10:17; Ps. 136:3)	"Lord of lords" (1 Tim. 6:15; Rev. 17:14; 19:16)
Unchanging and eternal (Ps. 90:2; 102:26–27; Mal. 3:6)	Unchanging and eternal (John 8:58; Col. 1:17; Heb. 1:11–12; 13:8)
Judge of all people (Gen. 18:25; Ps. 94:2; 96:13; 98:9)	Judge of all people (John 5:22; Acts 17:31; 2 Cor. 5:10; 2 Tim. 4:1)
Only Savior; no other God can save (Isa. 43:11; 45:21–22; Hos. 13:4)	Savior of the world; no salvation apart from him (John 4:42; Acts 4:12; Titus 2:13; 1 John 4:14)
Redeems from their sins a people for his own possession (Ex. 19:5; Ps. 130:7–8; Ezek. 37:23)	Redeems from their sins a people for his own possession (Titus 2:14)
Hears and answers prayers of those who call on him (Ps. 86:5–8; Isa. 55:6–7; Jer. 33:3; Joel 2:32)	Hears and answers prayers of those who call on him (John 14:14; Rom. 10:12–13; 1 Cor. 1:2; 2 Cor. 12:8–9)
Only God has divine glory (Isa. 42:8; 48:11)	Jesus has divine glory (John 17:5)
Worshiped by angels (Ps. 97:7)	Worshiped by angels (Heb. 1:6)

(Excerpt from *The Trinity* Rose Publishing, www.rose-publishing.com)

Mormonism

The Church of Jesus Christ
of Latter-day Saints

Some things you will learn in this session....

- The real story behind Joseph Smith's divine visions.

- What's inside the Book of Mormon.

- Why Mormon families often have many children.

- Who God was before he became "God" according to Mormon doctrine.

- Why you will not find any crosses on Mormon temples.

- What to say to Mormon missionaries in your neighborhood.

Session 4 Outline
Mormonism

1. Early Mormonism

    a. Joseph Smith, Jr. (1805–1844)

    - First Vision (Sacred Grove)

    - Visitations by Moroni

    - Moving to Ohio, Missouri, and Illinois

    - Assassination

    b. Brigham Young (1801–1877)

2. On what do Mormons base their beliefs?

    a. Four "standard works"

    - The Bible—King James Version

    - Book of Mormon

    - Doctrine and Covenants

    - Pearl of Great Price (Includes the Book of Abraham)

    b. Living prophets

3. Mormon teachings

    a. God is not a Trinity

    b. "Holy Ghost" (a personage); "holy spirit" (a fluid-like substance)

      c.   Jesus, "elder brother" and firstborn spirit child

      d.   Adam fell "up"; no sin nature

      e.   Afterlife

          • Three "degrees of glory" (Telestial, Terrestrial, Celestial)

          • Outer darkness

4.   Mormon practices

      a. "Word of Wisdom": no caffeine drinks, alcohol, tobacco

      b.   Temple rituals: endowments

      c.   Individual blood atonement

5.   What is the appeal of Mormonism?

      a.   Family emphasis

      b.   Social activities

      c.   Baptism on behalf of deceased relatives

6.   What does the Bible say?

      a. "even if an angel..."

          • Galatians 1:6–8

      b.   No gods before or after God

          • Isaiah 43:10; 40–45

      c.   God is not a man

          • Numbers 23:19; Hosea 11:9; Romans 1:22–23

      d.   Jesus Christ has always been God

- John 1:1

- Matthew 1; Luke 1

e. The gospel of salvation

- Romans 3:20–23; 6:23

- Ephesians 2:8–10

f. Jesus preserves his church

- Matthew 16:18

g. Testing prophets

- 1 John 4:1

- Deuteronomy 13:1–5; 18:21–22

7. Mormon missionaries at your door

a. Don't question their motives

b. Don't ridicule their beliefs

c. Don't let them pray for you

d. Don't agree to pray about the Book of Mormon; instead, test by Scripture

- Acts 17:11

e. Take them through the Scriptures

f. Tell them what Jesus has done for you

- 1 John 5:10–13

g. End on a positive note

Key Terms

Book of Abraham   Mormon scripture, now published as part of the Pearl of Great Price. In 1835 Joseph Smith purchased Egyptian artifacts from a traveling showman, announcing that they contained the writings of the biblical patriarch Abraham. The "translation" he produced, called the Book of Abraham, was debunked when papyri from the collection were rediscovered in 1967.

Book of Mormon   Mormon scripture said to have been translated by Joseph Smith from gold plates he received from the angel Moroni in 1827. It purports to tell the story of three people groups (the Lehites, Jaredites, and Mulekites) that migrated from the Middle East to the Americas, roughly between 2000 BC and AD 400. After being translated, the plates were taken back to heaven.

Celestial Kingdom   The highest of three heavenly "degrees of glory" awaiting faithful Latter-day Saints. Entrance into this kingdom is gained by complete obedience to the Mormon gospel, and those who reach its highest level become gods.

Doctrine and Covenants   Mormon scripture containing modern revelations, most given by Joseph Smith.

Endowment Ceremony   Secret temple ritual performed by living persons, sometimes on behalf of the dead. Required for exaltation.

Eternal Progression   Human progression starting from a pre-existent spirit, then into a human body, and then finally on to godhood.

Exaltation   Synonymous with eternal life. Only Mormons who gain exaltation have the ability to become gods and procreate throughout eternity.

Freemasonry (Masonic Lodge)   A secret society founded in London in the early 18th century. Known for its use of symbolism and secret rituals. Elements of Freemasonry are found in the Mormon temple endowment ceremony.

Inspired Version   Also known as the Joseph Smith Translation, this adaptation of the Bible was completed by Joseph Smith in 1833.

Lamanites and Nephites   According to the Book of Mormon, followers of Nephi and Laman, the sons of the Prophet Lehi who led his family to the New World prior to the capture of Jerusalem (c. 600 BC). Those who followed the wicked Laman were shown God's displeasure by being cursed with a dark skin (2 Nephi 5:21–25); they are considered the ancestors of the American Indians and Polynesians.

Moroni   Ancient Nephite leader who buried the gold plates containing the Book of Mormon and later appeared as an angel to Joseph Smith to tell him of their location. His image is found on many LDS temples throughout the world.

Pearl of Great Price   Mormon scripture containing the Book of Abraham, Book of Moses, and other short works.

Polygamy   Between 1852 and 1890 the practice of plural marriage became essential for any Mormon man hoping to achieve exaltation. The Mormon Church's sixth president had five wives and fathered 43 children. The Mormon Church renounced polygamy in 1890, and Utah was then granted statehood when anti-polygamy laws were written into the state constitution.

Priesthood   The basis on which Mormon males have power and authority to act on behalf of God. It consists of two orders: the Aaronic (or lesser) priesthood, and the Melchizedek priesthood. Males of African descent were denied the Mormon priesthood until 1978.

Telestial Kingdom   The lowest of three heavenly "degrees of glory" to which the worst sinners are sent to after death. The Holy Ghost will visit people in this kingdom, but the Father and Son will not.

Temples   Special buildings reserved for ordinances for the dead (including baptism for the dead), marriages for "time and eternity," and "sealings" of families for eternity.

Terrestrial Kingdom   The middle of three heavenly "degrees of glory," to which good people who are not Mormons are sent to after death. Jesus will visit people in this heaven, but God the Father will not.

Urim and Thummim   A translation device described by Joseph Smith as "two stones in silver bows." Allegedly received from Moroni together with the gold plates containing the text of the Book of Mormon. (Said to be the same as the Urim and Thummim mentioned in such biblical passages as Exodus 28:30.)

Word of Wisdom   Section 89 in Doctrine and Covenants which prohibits the consumption of caffeine drinks, alcohol, and tobacco.

Talk About It

Discussion Questions

1. Share about a conversation you had with a Mormon. What things were discussed? Was it easy or difficult to discuss different beliefs?

2. What are some reasons why people join the Mormon Church?

3. What was the purpose of Jesus' death and resurrection according to Mormonism? What was the purpose according to the Bible?

4. What difficulties and challenges do you think someone might face if he or she left the Mormon Church and became a Christian?

5. Do you feel ready to discuss your beliefs with Mormons? Why or why not? What would help you feel ready?

Get Into God's Word

Key Bible Verses

ℭ *Read Galatians 1:6–8*

Q   Why is belief in a "different gospel" so dangerous?

_____

_____

_____

ℭ *Read Matthew 16:16–18*

Q   What does Jesus promise about his church?

_____

_____

_____

ℭ *Read Romans 3:20–22*

Q   How are believers made righteous?

_____

_____

_____

Test Your Knowledge

Quick Quiz

1. Which of the following is *not* true about Joseph Smith, the founder of the Mormon Church?

   a. He claimed God commissioned him to restore the church on earth.
   b. He ran for president of the United States.
   c. He claimed that John the Baptist appeared to him.
   d. He was thrown in jail because he refused to stop preaching forgiveness.
   e. He "married" some of the wives of his colleagues.

2. True or False? The Mormon Church claims that the Book of Mormon is an historical record of ancient Hebraic peoples who came from the Middle East to the Americas.

3. According to Mormon teaching, Jesus was the eldest of God's spirit children and _____ was his younger, jealous brother.

4. According to the Bible, which of the following is true about salvation?
   a. Salvation cannot be earned by personal worthiness.
   b. Good works are the result of salvation, not its basis.
   c. Salvation is maintained by full obedience to the law.
   d. (a) and (b)
   e. All of the above

5. In Acts 17:11, the Berean Christians searched the _____ to test whether the Apostle Paul's message was from God.

(Answers on page 94)

Think About It

Personal Reflection

1. What attitude do I usually have toward Mormons? How have I treated Mormons whom I've known? How does God want me to treat them?

    _____

    _____

    _____

2. What can I do to be better prepared for when Mormon missionaries come knocking?

    _____

    _____

    _____

3. Do I have a friend, coworker, or family member who is a Mormon? If so, how can I be intentional about praying for them and looking for opportunities to tell them my testimony of what God has done in my life?

    _____

    _____

    _____

Reach Out

Witnessing Tips   (Do's and Don'ts)

- *Don't assume* that a Mormon defines a word in the same way you do.

- *Do define your terms*—and have them define theirs. (For example, "What do you believe about salvation? About eternal life? Are they the same, or different?")

- *Don't assume what an individual Mormon believes.* Not all Mormons agree with their leaders. This could be because they are not aware of what their leaders have taught. For example, if a Mormon appears to answer a question biblically, you may respond by saying something like, "That is exactly what the Bible teaches; however, are you aware that prophet so-and-so said just the opposite? Shouldn't they be in harmony with the Bible if they are getting their information from the same God who gave us the Bible?"

- *Do ask Mormons what they believe.* Rather than accusing, ask a question.

- *Don't dwell on topics that are especially sensitive to Mormons* and should only be addressed after they feel more comfortable discussing religious issues with you. Talking about the temple ceremony, the sacred garments, polygamy, or racism will almost certainly bring the discussion to a close. Use your time wisely.

- *Do concentrate on core issues.* What the Mormon believes about God the Father, Jesus Christ, and the Holy Spirit, as well as the issue of salvation, should be primary. Do your Mormon acquaintances have the assurance that when they die all of their sins are forgiven? Do they feel confident they will receive the best their religion has to offer (godhood, eternal increase)? If so, how so? If not, why not?

- *Don't be surprised if Mormons are suspicious of Christian literature.* Mormons often feel that information written about their church, but not by their church, is almost always inaccurate. If you do use Christian material, makes sure it is well-documented. Rather than insisting that the material is correct, have

Mormons show you where the information could be wrong. To do this they will need to read the material and check the references.

- *Do memorize certain points and quotes.* This often works better than using printed material because it shows the Mormon that you have taken the time to read LDS resources. Quote directly from LDS sources if possible. Statements from LDS leaders work best.

- *Don't think you need to cover every topic in one sitting.* Sometimes dealing with one or two subjects makes it easier to remember what you talked about.

- *Do be patient.* Mormons are led to believe that leaving the LDS church will lead to damnation. This is not a decision most Mormons make in an instant.

(Excerpt from *10 Q&A on Mormonism* Rose Publishing, www.rose-publishing.com)

Learn More

Joseph Smith: Prophet or Fraud?

"Joseph Smith, the Prophet and Seer of the Lord, has done more, save Jesus only, for the salvation of men in this world, than any other man that ever lived in it." —*Doctrine and Covenants* 135:3

Joseph Smith denounced the Trinity:

"Many men say there is one God; the Father, the Son and the Holy Ghost are only one God! I say that is a strange God anyhow—three in one, and one in three! It is a curious organization. All are to be crammed into one God, according to sectarianism. It would make the biggest God in all the world. He would be a wonderfully big God—he would be a giant or a monster."—*Teachings of the Prophet Joseph Smith*, p. 372

Joseph Smith boasted that he accomplished more than the apostles or Jesus:

"I have more to boast of than ever any man had. I am the only man that has ever been able to keep a whole church together since the days of Adam. A large majority of the whole have stood by me. Neither Paul, John, Peter, nor Jesus ever did it. I boast that no man ever did such a work as I. The followers of Jesus ran away from Him; but the Latter-day Saints never ran away from me yet."—*History of the Church*, Vol. 6, pp. 408–412

Mormonism stands or falls on Joseph Smith:

"Mormonism, as it is called, *must stand or fall on the story of Joseph Smith.* He was either a prophet of God, divinely called, properly appointed and commissioned, or he was one of the biggest frauds this world has ever seen. *There is no middle ground.*"—Mormon prophet Joseph Fielding Smith, *Doctrines of Salvation*, Vol. 1, p. 188 (italics in original)

No salvation without Joseph Smith:

> "If it had not been for Joseph Smith and the restoration, there would be no salvation."—Mormon apostle Bruce R. McConkie, *Mormon Doctrine* (1978), p. 670

> "I know that Joseph Smith is a Prophet of God, that this is the Gospel of salvation, and if you do not believe it you will be damned, every one of you."—Mormon prophet Brigham Young, *Journal of Discourses*, Vol. 4, p. 298

> "... no man or woman in this dispensation will ever enter into the celestial kingdom of God without the consent of Joseph Smith."—Brigham Young, *Journal of Discourses*, Vol. 7, p. 289

❡ Notes

Eastern Spirituality

Hinduism, Buddhism, and the New Age

Some things you will learn in this session....

- What makes Hinduism and Buddhism different—and yet alike.

- The story of the first Buddha.

- Why the New Age is popular in the West.

- What people are really seeking through meditation and yoga.

- Why reincarnation is not just a "fun idea" about past lives.

Session 5 Outline
Eastern Spirituality

1. Eastern religions' arrival and impact in North America

    a. Swami Vivekananda –1893

    b. Paramahansa Yogananda—1920

    c. Oriental Exclusion Act—ended 1965

    d. New Age Movement—1980s

2. Three common threads

    a. Pantheism

    b. Reincarnation, karma

    c. Yoga, meditation

3. Hinduism

    a. Hindu scriptures (Four Vedas, Upanishads, Bhagavad Gita)

    b. Polytheism; Brahman-Atman

    c. Salvation in Hinduism

    d. Three major expressions

        • Vaishnavism

- Shaivism

- Shaktism

4. Buddhism

    a.   Siddhartha Gautama

    b.   No God is needed

    c.   Four Noble Truths

- Suffering

- Ignorance

- Nirvana

- Eightfold Path

    d.   Three major expressions

- Theravada ("path of the elders")

- Mahayana ("greater vehicle")

- Vajrayana ("diamond vehicle")

5. New Age Movement

    a.   Transcendentalism, spiritualism, Theosophy

    b.   Rejection of traditional Christianity

    c.   What is the attraction?

- Personal godhood

- Freedom to explore

- Rejecting traditional religious approaches

- Techniques for enlightenment

- Physical healing

- Planetary transformation

6. How do we apply the Bible?

   a. The one true God is personal and distinct from his creation

      - Genesis 1; Romans 1

   b. Jesus is the unique redeemer

      - 1 Timothy 2:5; Matthew 7:13; John 14:6

   c. Reincarnation undermines justice

      - Hebrews 9:27

   d. Resurrection, not reincarnation

      - John 5:28

      - John 6:40

      - Philippians 3:10

   e. Christian meditation is about attachment to God

      - Psalm 48:9

Key Terms

Bhagavad Gita   (c. AD 100) One of the best-known sacred writings of Hinduism, an epic poem whose central figure is the deity Krishna.

Bodhisattva   ("enlightened existence," "awakened being") One who aspires to buddhahood but postpones his own enlightenment to alleviate the suffering of others by his own merits.

Brahman-Atman   In Hinduism, Brahman is the Divine Totality, the ultimate reality, and Atman is the individual soul, like a spark from the huge fire of Brahman. God is not a personal creator, distinct from his creation, but both the creature and its source are part of the same "big reality," called Brahman-Atman.

Enlightenment   ("awakening") The realization that souls have the illusion of being reincarnated and floating through eternity, bound in ignorance and suffering senselessly in one body after another.

Four Vedas   ("knowledge") The earliest Hindu texts, written approximately 1500–1000 BC.

Guru   ("teacher") The highest rank of spiritual teacher in Hinduism, Jainism and Sikhism. One who has attained enlightenment or salvation after thousands of reincarnations.

Hare Krishna   The International Society for Krishna Consciousness (ISKCON), founded in New York in 1966 by Swami Prabhubada (1896–1977). Vaishnava sect whose followers became known for their saffron robes, dancing on city streets, and aggressive fundraising techniques.

Hindu Countermission   A response by Hindus to Christian missionary efforts in which gurus are sent abroad to convert Westerners.

Karma   ("act") The spiritual principle of cause and effect, in which some kind of reward or punishment follows one's every act, whether good or bad. Thus, in Hinduism a person's past actions govern his present life, and future lives (reincarnations) are determined by past and present actions.

Mahayana   ("greater vehicle") Branch of Buddhism emphasizing that all may attain the essential Buddha-nature through meditation and the aid of bodhisattvas.

Maya Illusion, unreality, dream. The power that causes people to believe in the false idea of duality or the phenomenal (material) world.

Moksha ("liberation") Release or salvation in Hinduism.

Nirvana ("extinction") The final liberation in Buddhism. Literally means "blowing out," like a candle flame. The end of all personal existence.

Noble Eightfold Path In Buddhism, it is the means by which one pursues release from transcience and suffering, with nirvana as the ultimate goal. Consists of right understanding, thoughts, speech, action, livelihood, endeavor, mindfulness, and concentration.

Oriental Exclusion Act (1924) Severely restricted immigration from Asia to the United States. After it ended in 1965, many representatives of eastern religions began proselytizing in the U.S.

Pantheism (Greek *pan*, "all," and *theos*, "God") The teaching that God is not separate from his creation, but a vague impersonal force.

Paramahansa Yogananda (1893–1952) Founded the Self-Realization Fellowship in 1920. Most famous for his book Autobiography of a Yogi (1946).

Polytheism (*poly* "many," *theos* "God") The belief in many gods. This is the most common form of ancient religion found worldwide, and still exists today in many forms.

Reincarnation Each soul is reborn literally thousands of times before achieving liberation, or salvation. (Also called transmigration or metempsychosis.)

Samsara ("flow together") The wandering that is the fate of the soul over many reincarnations.

Shaivism A Hindu tradition with multiple expressions. The most significant, Shaiva Siddhanta, is theistic rather than impersonalistic.

Shaktism A Hindu tradition emphasizing devotion to Shakti or the Devi (the divine mother) as the ultimate expression of the godhead.

Swami Vivekananda (1863–1902) Indian devotee of Ramakrishna who famously introduced Hinduism to many Americans through his appearance at the World's Parliament of Religions in 1893.

Tantrism A philosophy in Hinduism and Buddhism which emphasizes union of male and female principles through a variety of ritual techniques, including sexual intercourse.

Theravada ("path of the elders") Branch of Buddhism emphasizing Samadhi ("concentration") meditation and Vipassana ("insight") meditation. Strongly affirms the existence of the historical Buddha ("Sakyamuni").

Transcendental Meditation (TM) Maharishi Mahesh Yogi (1917–2008) founded the TM movement in India in 1957 (as the Spiritual Regeneration Movement). TM emphasizes a "mechanical" path to enlightenment. Gained early popularity through the Yogi's association with the Beatles, the Beach Boys, and other entertainers in the 1960s.

Upanishads Over 100 Hindu philosophical treatises written approximately 800–500 BC.

Vaishnavism A Hindu tradition that emphasizes the worship of Vishnu. Understands Brahman in terms of more personal manifestations (such as Ram and Krishna, hero of the Bhagavad Gita).

Vajrayana ("diamond vehicle") Branch of Buddhism made popular in the West by the Dalai Lama. Combines Mahayana, Indian Tantra, and the occultic Bön religion of ancient Tibet (which promotes the worship of dark spirits). Shingon Buddhism in Japan is derived from Vajrayana.

Yoga and Meditation Physical and mental practices developed as ways of reducing one's karma—the attachment to the physical world and our individual selves.

Zen Buddhism Imported from China and established as a separate school in Japan in the 12th century. Emphasizes sudden and spontaneous enlightenment—the experience of one's true nature.

Talk About It

Discussion Questions

1. After watching this session, what did you learn about eastern spirituality that you didn't know or misunderstood before?

2. Share about a time when you had an interaction or conversation with someone in an eastern religion. What did you learn from that experience?

3. How would you describe Jesus of Christianity to someone who believes Jesus was a guru or an enlightened person (bodhisattva)?

4. How would you respond to someone who says this? "Eastern religions and Christianity are basically the same. They're just different paths to escaping pain and getting to God."

5. What difficulties and challenges do you think someone who is a follower of an eastern religion would face if he or she became a Christian?

Get Into God's Word

Key Bible Verses

♪ *Read Hebrews 9:27*

Q   What does this verse reveal about the afterlife?

_____

_____

_____

♪ *Read John 14:6*

Q   How many ways are there to God? What—or who—is the way to God?

_____

_____

_____

♪ *Read Psalm 48:9 and Psalm 1:2*

Q   What is the focus of Christian meditation?

_____

_____

_____

Test Your Knowledge

Quick Quiz

1. At the root of much of today's "spirituality" is _____, an ancient religion.

    a. Buddhism
    b. Hinduism
    c. Theravada
    d. Astrology

2. True or False? In Buddhism, there is a creator behind the reality of the cosmos that explains it.

3. The New Age movement:

    a. Rejects sin as the ultimate cause of evil.
    b. Emphasizes personal autonomy.
    c. Accepts pantheism.
    d. (a) and (b)
    e. All of the above

4. In eastern spiritual meditation, a person is seeking to _____.

    a. pay for their sins
    b. vanish
    c. be resurrected
    d. hear God

5. The Bible teaches that Jesus Christ alone is the _____ between the one, holy God and sinful human beings.

(Answers on page 94)

Personal Reflection

1. Is my meditation about moving closer to God, or is it about detachment from life?

   _____

   _____

   _____

2. Do I know the Bible well enough to show someone the uniqueness of the life and claims of Jesus Christ?

   _____

   _____

   _____

3. Pray for someone you know who is involved in an eastern religion or the New Age. When and how do you think God might be leading you to share the gospel with this person?

   _____

   _____

   _____

Reach Out

Witnessing Tips (Do's and Don'ts)

- *Do familiarize yourself with the basic teachings* of the type of Hinduism or Buddhism or teachings your friend follows.

- *Do ask questions* about your friend's personal beliefs (which may be different from what is commonly taught by their religious group).

- *Don't be quick to criticize your friend's religion* (or native culture) or engage in debates. You can encourage their trust and respect through personal kindness and your focus on Christ.

- *Do "be prepared to give an answer"* and explain "the reason for the hope that you have" (1 Peter 3:15). Know what you believe and why—and back it up from Scripture.

- *Don't overlook potentially sensitive cultural factors* that may be important to your friend, such as modest dress or a vegetarian diet.

- *Do share your personal testimony* of trusting in Christ for salvation. As appropriate, point your friend to the testimonies of Hindus/Buddhists/New Agers who have become Christians.

- *Do encourage your Hindu/Buddhist friend to read the Gospel of John* and be prepared to discuss it with him or her.

- *Do encourage New Age friends to read what the Bible says about Jesus* and clarify the meanings of scriptural terms (such as "Christ") that New Age writers commonly redefine.

- *Don't forget to pray faithfully* that God will draw your friend to Christ by the Holy Spirit.

The Dalai Lama

Tenzin Gyatso (1935–), the 14th Dalai Lama ("ocean of wisdom"), was born in rural Tibet. A monk of the Gelug ("Yellow Hat") sect of Tibetan Buddhism, he is said to be the reincarnation of the previous thirteen Dalai Lamas, the god-kings of Tibet (considered manifestations of Avalokitesvara, the bodhisattva of compassion). In 1959, he fled Tibet because of conflict with the ruling Chinese, and now heads the Tibetan government in exile in Dharamsala, India.

The Dalai Lama has done far more than anyone else to popularize Tibetan Buddhism in the West, cultivating well-publicized friendships with celebrities. But there is more to the story. In 2001 the Dalai Lama told an interviewer for Christianity Today that "Jesus Christ also lived previous lives," adding that Jesus "reached a high state, either as a Bodhisattva, or an enlightened person, through Buddhist practice or something like that."

In *A Guide to Cults and New Religions* (InterVarsity, 2005), researcher James Stephens notes that Tibetan Buddhism uses "a rigorous system of works righteousness" to enable followers to accumulate sufficient merit to "achieve deliverance from the ... cycle of rebirths. These works include reciting mantras and sutras, ... deity yoga, utilizing Buddhist rosary beads, prayer wheels, prayer flags and mani stones, visualizing demonic entities, and making symbolic offerings." Few people realize that the Dalai Lama's religion is also deeply occultic, thanks in part to the influence of the ancient Bön religion. The Dalai Lama consults the demon-possessed Nechung Oracle for state decisions, and the Tantrism of Tibetan Buddhism includes the ritual use of human remains and of bodily excretions known as the "five ambrosias."

(Adapted from *Christianity & Eastern Religions* Rose Publishing, www.rose-publishing.com)

❧ Notes

℅ *Notes*

Islam

Some things you will learn in this session....

- The story of Muhammad's encounter with the angel Gabriel.

- Why Mecca is a most holy place for Muslims.

- What Muslims believe about Jesus and the Gospels.

- The difference between Jihad and Jihadism.

- What attracts converts to Islam.

- What you need to know when talking with Muslims

Session 6 Outline
Islam

1. Life of Muhammad

    a. Born in Mecca (AD 570)

    b. First encounter with Gabriel (AD 610)

    c. Journey to Medina (AD 622); Hijrah

    d. Conquest of Mecca (AD 630)

    e. Died in Medina (AD 632)

2. Scriptures and guiding documents

    a. The Qur'an

    b. The Bible—considered corrupted

    c. Sunnah (Hadith, Sira)

3. Six Beliefs

    a. Allah

    b. Prophets—including

        • Muhammad

        • Jesus

    c. Angels (and jinn)

    d. Holy books (Qur'an, Torah, Psalms, Gospels)

    e. Day of judgment

    f. Fate

4. Five Pillars

    a. Profession of faith (Shahadah)

    b. Prayers (Salat)

    c. Almsgiving (Zakat)

    d. Fasting (Sawm)

    e. Pilgrimage to Mecca (Hajj)

5. Salvation

    a. No concept of original sin

    b. Obedience through repentance and human effort

    c. Two kinds of jihad

- Greater jihad (internal struggle to live a righteous life)

- Lesser jihad (holy war in defense of Islam)

6. Three major expressions

    a. Sunni

    b. Shi'a

    c. Sufi

    d. Other expressions

- Folk Islam

- Islamism

- Jihadism

- Bahá'í Faith

- Nation of Islam

7. The appeal of Islam

   a. Simplicity of beliefs and requirements

   b. Moral clarity

   c. All-encompassing nature

   d. Universal brotherhood

8. What does the Bible say?

   a. Romans 5:8

   b. 1 John 4:10

9. How to approach Muslims

   a. Be knowledgeable about Islam and Christianity

   b. Draw them out

   c. Emphasize Christianity is a relationship with God

   d. Be culturally sensitive

   e. Appreciate the high cost of leaving Islam

   f. Bear in mind that it's all about Muhammad

Key Terms

Arianism   Originated in the fourth century AD and argues that Jesus does not share the same essence with God, and thus does not share in the same divine nature with eternity and authority. The Nicene, Chalcedonian, and Athanasian Creeds are primarily responses to this heresy.

Bahá'í Faith   Founded in 1844 in Iran. Teaches that God has revealed himself through nine "manifestations" including Adam, Moses, Krishna, Buddha, Jesus, Muhammad, and Bahá'u'lláh. There are an estimated 8 million Bahá'ís worldwide.

Hadith   A report of a saying or behavior of Muhammad which sets a precedent for Muslim practice and becomes the basis of shari'a.

Hajj   The annual pilgrimage to Mecca.

Hijrah   Muhammad's flight from Mecca to Medina in AD 622 which marks the first year in the Islamic calendar.

Injil   The "book given to Jesus," similar to the Greek word *evangel*, meaning "good news." Muslims do not believe that no Injil remains on earth that hasn't been corrupted. Christians often refer to the Gospels, or a single Gospel, as "the Injil" when conversing with Muslims.

Islamism   Broad movement promoting the idea that full and correct implementation of Islam worldwide requires both political power and state control. Sometimes called fundamentalism or Salafism.

Jihad   ("holy fighting") A spiritual struggle that can either be internal (striving in one's soul to do right) or external (an effort against the enemies of Islam).

Jihadism   A radical Islamic ideology. It views Western democracy as a violation of tawheed and an offense to God, and creation of a perfect Islamic state by violent means as necessary.

Jinn   (also "Genie") A type of supernatural, personal being—distinct from humans and demons—said to have been made by Allah from smokeless fire. Jinn can be either helpful or harmful to mankind.

Kaaba (Ka'bah)   The cube-shaped structure in Mecca toward which all Muslims must pray. Believed to have been an altar used by Abraham.

Mecca   The center of idol worship in AD 610 when Muhammad first challenged the people to forsake idolatry and embrace Islam. Most Meccans rejected his message, and many began to persecute the early Muslims, causing them to flee (hijra) to the town of Medina in AD 622. Located in what is now Saudi Arabia.

Nation of Islam   Founded in 1930 in Detroit, Michigan by Wallace D. Fard. Currently led by Louis Farrakhan. Affirms belief in Allah and the Qur'an, but also teaches that millions of "Allahs" have lived and died since creation, and collectively the black race is God. Master Fard is considered the Supreme Allah and Savior.

Qur'an (Koran)   ("recitation") Revealed to Muhammad by the angel Gabriel over a period of 22 years. In AD 632 the recitations were collected together to become the Qur'an. Considered divine in its original Arabic.

Salat   A set ritual of prayer to be done five specific times every day (sometimes combined in three sessions), memorized in Arabic, with ritual washings before each sequence. The head must be covered, the body pointed toward Mecca, and the motions and prostrations must be followed for the prayers to be valid.

Shahadah   The foundational Muslim profession of faith: "There is no God but Allah, and Muhammad is his prophet."

Shari'a   ("way," "path") Islamic religious law, based upon the Sunnah. The four schools of Sunni interpretation are named after their founders: Hanafi (d. 767), Maliki (d. 795), Shafi'i (d. 820), and Hanbali (d. 855). Shi'ia Muslims also have schools of their own.

Shi'a (Shi'ite)   (from Arabic Shi'ati Ali, "party of Ali") A minority of Muslims (10% worldwide) which believes that the proper successor to Muhammad should be his blood relative, beginning with Ali, his son-in-law. The Sunni-Shi'a split happened shortly after Muhammad's death in a violent dispute about who should lead the Muslim community. Shi'a follow ten central practices which include the Five Pillars. Many believe in a series of 12 imams serving as Muhammad's spiritual and political successors. The final one will someday appear with Jesus.

Shirk   ("associating") Committing blasphemy by assigning partners or equals to Allah, thereby compromising his uniqueness.

Sira   (from Arabic Sirah Rasul Allah, "life of the messenger of God") Biographies of Muhammad that provide interpretive insights about his life and the early history of Islam.

Sufism   A mystical form of Islam, often viewed as one of its distinct branches but which has both Sunni or Shi'a followers. Emphasis is placed on experiential knowledge of God, sometimes by trances induced through chanting the names of Allah or dancing (as seen in "whirling dervishes").

Sunnah Literally: the "trodden path" of Muhammad and his close companions. The Sunnah (Muhammad's examples) becomes the basis for shari'a.

Sunni (from Arabic Ahl as-Sunnah, "people of the tradition") The majority of Muslims (90% worldwide) identify themselves in contrast to the Shi'a. The Sunni-Shi'a split began shortly after Muhammad's death in a violent dispute about who should lead the Muslim community. Sunni hold to the Five Pillars and the Six Beliefs. Many believe that a figure from Muhammad's family, known as the Mahdi, will appear with Jesus before the final judgment.

Tawheed (Tawhid)   ("oneness") The central doctrine of Allah's absolute oneness and uniqueness.

Talk About It

Discussion Questions

1. After watching this session, what did you learn about Islam that you didn't know or understand before?

2. Share about a time that you had an interaction or conversation with a Muslim. What did you learn from that experience?

3. How is salvation in Islamic teaching different than what Jesus taught about how to be saved?

4. How is the gospel of Jesus Christ good news for Muslims?

5. Read 1 Corinthians 9:19–23. How can you apply theses verses in your own conversations and interactions with Muslims?

Get Into God's Word

Key Bible Verses

☙ *Read Romans 8:15–17*

Q   According to this passage, what is the result of receiving the "Spirit of sonship"?

_____

_____

_____

☙ *Read Hebrews 4:14–16*

Q   According to this passage, why can believers "approach the throne of grace with confidence"?

_____

_____

_____

☙ *Read Romans 5:8–10 and 1 John 4:10*

Q   According to these two passages, on what do believers base their assurance that they will be saved from God's wrath?

_____

_____

_____

Test Your Knowledge

Quick Quiz

1. Which of the following is *not* taught in Islam?

    a. The Qur'an which people have today is a copy of an eternal tablet in heaven.s

    b. The Torah, Psalms, and Gospels have been corrupted.

    c. "Allah" refers to the Fatherhood of God.

    d. Muhammad was the greatest man who ever lived.

2. True or False? The entire Qur'an was composed by Muhammad during the angel Gabriel's first visit.

3. Islam teaches that salvation depends upon:

    a. A person's good deeds outweighing their bad deeds.

    b. The will of Allah.

    c. Both of the above

    d. None of the above

4. True or False? In the final analysis Islam is all about Muhammad—what Muhammad says about God and what Muhammad would do in any situation.

5. Islam is a religion of works and merit, but according to the Bible, good works are the _____ of salvation—not the means of attaining it.

(Answers on page 94)

Think About It

Personal Reflection

1. What can I do to become more knowledgeable about Islam and Christianity?

    _____

    _____

    _____

2. What steps can I take toward developing a relationship with someone I know who is a Muslim? How might God be leading me to one day share the gospel of grace with them?

    _____

    _____

    _____

3. If I have only limited contact with Muslims, what can I do to support ministries or missionaries that reach out to Muslims?

    _____

    _____

    _____

Witnessing Tips   (Do's and Don'ts)

- *Do make it clear you are a follower of Christ,* by your loving words and righteous lifestyle.

- *Don't assume your Muslim friend understands what you mean* when you say "Christian."

- *Do take time to build a relationship.* Practice hospitality.

- *Don't be surprised if you are rejected at first.* It is best to offer Muslim friends store-bought sweets and to avoid anything with pork or alcohol.

- *Do approach your encounters as a learner.* Ask questions.

- *Don't take notes* and treat Muslim friends like an academic project.

- *Do correct their misunderstandings* of your beliefs.

- *Don't argue.* If they want to debate with a Christian, refer them to the web site www.debate.org.uk

- *Do talk about Jesus.* Use his title, Isa Al Masih.

- *Don't insult* the prophet Muhammad.

- *Do pray out loud with your Muslim friends.* Ask if you can pray for their practical needs, healing, and worries. Look for opportunities and pray in Jesus' name.

- *Don't start your prayer with "Our Father…"* because Muslims misunderstand the fatherhood of God (as sexual). Wait until you correct this misunderstanding before using "Father" or "Abba." At first address your prayer to "Almighty God" or "Lord God."

- *Do use your right hand* in giving and receiving gifts.

- *Don't use your left hand for eating food* (especially when learning to eat with your hands). The left hand is used for toilet cleaning; the right hand for eating.

- *Do treat your Bible with respect.* Store it high on a shelf. Some wrap it in a beautiful cloth.

- *Don't put your Bible on the floor or in the bathroom* as reading material. Many Muslims are superstitious about the bathroom.

- *Do be gender-sensitive:* interact man to man, woman to woman.

- *Don't allow any compromising situation*, even just to protect from a possible rumor. An Arab proverb says, "A man and woman alone together are three with the devil."

- *Do be careful with your body language.* Remove your shoes when entering a home or place of prayer (especially if you see shoes at the threshold).

- *Don't sit so that the sole of your foot or shoe is facing someone.* Women, don't look men directly in the eye, or at least quickly avert your glance.

- *Do practice modesty,* even among Westernized Muslims. For women this is especially important, since family honor is tied to their behavior and reputation.

- *Don't assume that Muslims think the same as you do,* even if they dress the same.

(Excerpt from *Islam & Christianity* Rose Publishing, www.rose-publishing.com)

Comparing Beliefs about the Afterlife

	What Muslims Believe	What Christians Believe
Judgment Day	Everyone should fear judgment day, in which each person's deeds will be weighed on a scale. Each person has two "recording angels" who keep a list of every deed, both good and bad. Islamic teachers assign credits to deeds related to the pillars of Islam. It is unthinkable for many Muslims to abandon their accumulation of credits and trust a savior.	After death, all people await the final judgment when both believers and unbelievers will be resurrected. All will be judged according to the deeds they have done, but believers will be saved because God removed the record that contained the charges against them. He destroyed it by nailing it to the cross of Jesus (Colossians 2:14).
Salvation	In Islam, there is no savior. Salvation is possible, for Allah can always forgive (his will is supreme)—but he is primarily the judge. There are many descriptive warnings about hellfire and punishment in the Qur'an. Jihadists use the Qur'an to teach that paradise is guaranteed for their martyrs. Most Muslim scholars and leaders reject the terrorists' definitions of jihad and martyrdom.	Even if one's list of good deeds outweighed their list of bad deeds, it would not make them acceptable to God. The Bible says this would only cause boasting and pride, as though someone could impress God by their good deeds (Ephesians 2:8–10). Instead, God has credited believers with the righteousness of Christ, so salvation is a gift, not earned by anyone—not even martyrs—but bought with a great price (Jesus' blood).
Paradise	The Qur'an says, "For those who reject Allah, there is a terrible penalty: but for those who believe and work righteous deeds, there is forgiveness and a magnificent reward" (Surah 35:7). This great reward is janna, a garden paradise, an eternal place of both sensual and spiritual pleasures.	God the Father adopts those he saves into his family so they may live forever with Jesus in heaven. To be saved involves being "born again" into a new relationship with God (John 3:5).

(Adapted from *Islam & Christianity* Rose Publishing, www.rose-publishing.com)

ℭ Notes

Notes

Quiz Answer Keys

SESSION 1

1. b
2. False
3. e
4. True
5. enemies (or adversaries)

SESSION 2

1. e
2. True
3. d
4. False
5. grace

SESSION 3

1. d
2. True
3. c
4. False
5. questions

SESSION 4

1. d
2. True
3. Lucifer
4. d
5. Scriptures

SESSION 5

1. b
2. False
3. e
4. b
5. mediator

SESSION 6

1. c
2. False
3. c
4. True
5. fruit (or outcome, result)

Four Views of the End Times
DVD-Based Study
For Individual or Group Use

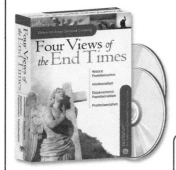

Complete *Four Views of the End Times* DVD-Based Study Kit
• Contains one each of everything below
ISBN: 9781596364127

Four Views of the End Times DVD-Based Study Leader Pack
• All six DVD-based sessions
• Leader Guide on disc as a printable PDF
• Fliers, bulletin inserts, posters and banners as PDFs on disc
ISBN: 9781596364240

Leader Guide
• Leader Guide gives step-by-step instructions for group hosts or facilitators so you don't have to be the expert
ISBN: 9781596364257

Participant Guide
• Each participant will need a guide
• Guide contains definitions, charts, comparisons, Bible references, discussion questions, and more
ISBN: 9781596364264

Four Views of the End Times pamphlet – fold-out chart
• Side-by-side comparison chart compares 4 views
• 12-page pamphlet fits in the back of a Bible cover
• Perfect for quick reference; includes color diagrams of each view
• Contains Scripture references for each view
• Lists names of notable Christians who support each view
ISBN: 9781596360891

PowerPoint® presentation
• Contains more than 100 slides to expand the scope of the teaching

ISBN: 9781596363014

fourviewsoftheendtimes.com

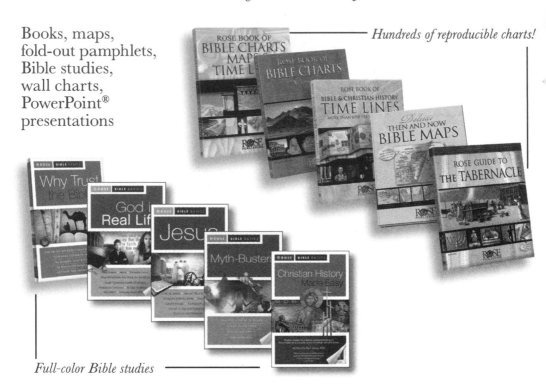